D1807861

Memory Aids to Your Great Adventure

by Russ Crowley

Published by Russ Crowley

Memory Aids To Your Great Adventure

www.learnthaialphabet.com

Copyright © 2013 by Russ Crowley

ISBN 978-1-908203-04-5 (paperback own ISBN)
ISBN 978-1492128892 (paperback CreateSpace ISBN)
ISBN 978-1-908203-03-8 (ebk)

All translations by Duangta Wanthong Mondi
All illustrations by Toni Howard
Front cover by Russ Crowley & Toni Howard
Rear cover by Russ Crowley

Table of Contents

The Thai Alphabet

You've decided to make the step to learn the Thai alphabet, you've settled down with your study book, read the introduction chapter, you know how best to use the book and you begin learning Thai. Fantastic news!

Four or five days later, you realise that the only way you're going to be able to learn and retain the alphabet is by using 'flash cards'. You either make our own or purchase some of the excellent cards available in Thailand, great stuff!

You work through the Middle Class consonants and learn all 9, then you move on to the High Class consonants (there are 11 of these) and then onto the final set, Low Class.

You've cracked it, you can now recognise all of the 44 consonants in the Thai alphabet. You start reading some 'easier' words in Thai and then, hang-on! I don't understand that word. That consonant at the end should be an /s/ sound, yet the girl speaking on the mp3 is pronouncing it like /t/?

Confused? It's a fairly common occurrence but the situation occurs because some Thai consonants have a different sound depending on whether they are an *initial consonant* or a *final consonant*.

You have to learn these and it's not particularly easy: to be honest with you, it can drive you barmy; it can take a while and banging your head against the wall will probably, in all sincerity, not really help.

There is a way though! This book will help you to learn, in a very easy, quick and logical method, the sounds the consonants and vowels of the Thai Alphabet make.

Introduction

I read '*How to Learn Any Language"* by *Barry Farber* a few years ago and one of the excellent techniques that he covers is *Harry Lorayne's, Magic Memory Aid*. This is a trick where you use acronyms, mnemonics and associations with an event, fictitious or otherwise that helps you recall that information.

It's a brilliant method because if you can create the association yourself then it becomes even more memorable, is easier to recall, and just sticks in your head.

There's one particular example that I use to explain for myself and that's how I always used to get the Thai words for *school* and *hotel* mixed up: one is called *rong raem* and the other is *rong rian*; but, which is which?

Well, *school is rong rian* and *hotel* is *rong raem* (this sounds quite close to *rong rem*, but stretch the 'rem' part out).

I always had difficulty remembering which was which until I came up with this 'scenario': I remember being on a rugby tour a few years ago and after the conclusion of the days antics, visualised getting back to the hotel late at night in the dark and accidently entering the *'wrong room'* - *rong rem*. From this I get *hotel* / *rong rem* / *wrong room* - simple!

Okay, you may be thinking this is a bit lame, but this is the beauty of this kind of association, it only needs to be a tenuous link and the chances are you will never forget it.

How Do We Do It?

Fortunately for you though, I'm not going to give you lots of anecdotes or stories to help you remember. I'm actually going to make it even simpler by giving you pictures instead; this makes it far easier to remember and it will embed itself in your mind.

Now my assumption is that you're reading this book because you're struggling to learn the Thai alphabet sounds. Notice I don't say *'learn the Thai alphabet'* - if you've learnt the names of all the consonants then I would find it strange you getting this book. By the way, did I tell you the main reason why I wrote *Learning Thai, Your Great Adventure*? Yep! I couldn't remember the consonant names or their order so, to solve those problems, I decided to write it all down.

Anyway, the alphabet sounds...

We'll start with the consonants as you have to learn these before you go onto the vowels. You've probably realised that the Thai alphabet is different to the English alphabet in a number of ways. The first, and most obvious is the script. Now don't cringe, it may look daunting but you can do it.

How do I know you can do it? Simply because I did it. I failed miserably at French, Spanish and German and I knew their alphabets! And if I can learn Thai, then so can **anyone**.

The second thing you may be aware of is that in the Thai alphabet, consonants and vowels don't mix. In the Roman alphabet, we have A, B, C, D, E, F...and the vowels are right in there, 5 out of 26.

Confusing for a lot of non-native Brits is the sounds of these: these 5 vowels make something like 19 different sounds between them (plus we've got the consonants which sound like vowels, such as *i* as in *heavy* [*hev'i*]) so the problems aren't all one way.

Fortunately though, in Thai, consonants and vowels don't mix, they stay separate - this is a good thing. The bad news though is there are 44 consonants and 32 vowels; but, we like challenges and the fact that some of the consonants make different sounds when in a different syllable position doesn't bother us in the slightest. Also the fact that Thai is a tonal language and we therefore have to learn and remember whether each consonant is Low class, Middle class or High class doesn't put us off either. Do you know why? Because we have a plan. It's not just any old plan though, it's a cunning one!

It works because the simple picture has everything in it to tell you what you need to know.

So, rather than me telling you I'm walking down a dark corridor, fumbling for my key, groping for the door handle...the key doesn't work, try again, make lots of noise...you get the idea. It takes a while for me to tell you this but if I have a picture which shows all of the information, I can then recall this picture far faster than going through the process I have just mentioned. This is how we teach you the information you need.

For example, the first letter of the Thai alphabet is ก . As a beginner, you're not that interested in what it's actually called (though this is important, you can work on it later), you just want to know what sounds it makes so you can begin speaking and reading Thai.

If you were paying attention you'll have noticed I said sound**s**, not sound. This particular consonant makes two different sounds: it makes one sound when it's the initial consonant of a syllable and it makes another totally different sound when it's a final or end consonant of a syllable.

Even more horrified? I hope not! Remember, we still have our cunning plan...

I personally think that you can learn the consonants in a few hours on one day and then learn the vowels the next day. If you then spread it about over a few days I am 100% sure you can easily grasp everything in this book within a few days. If you have a photographic memory, you're laughing but, if like me, you have a normal memory, it will take a little longer.

Method

Right then, how do we do it?

Here we have a picture of a knight. Now this knight is not just any old knight, he's actually one of the most virtuous and famous knights of them all: it's Galahad, one of King Arthur's knights from the Arthurian Legend of King Arthur and his Round Table.

But, '*Galahad, a knight of King Arthur and his Round Table*' is a bit of a mouthful to remember so we'll shorten it to something easier: Galahad Knight.

This is the name for this gallant warrior: **Galahad Knight**.

Now, *Galahad Knight* provides us with all the information we need to be able to recognise the Thai consonant - ก .

It also gives us the initial consonant sound and the final consonant sound. How?

To show you, we superimpose the Thai consonant shape ก onto the image.

This then gives us:

That's not 100% clear so, we'll zoom in a little bit:

Now you can see how the shape of the consonant conforms to the front-edge of Galahad Knights' shield, his torso and his helmet:

even where the visor on the helmet matches the '*beak*' of the consonant.

This is all you need to remember the sounds the first letter of the Thai alphabet makes. How does this help us?

- Well, from the picture name, we take the initial letter of the first word to be the sound the consonant makes when it's an **initial consonant**: Galahad

- The initial letter of the second word is the sound the consonant makes when it's a **final consonant**: Knight.

ก makes the **G** sound (or /**g**/ sound) when it's acting as an initial consonant, and it makes the **K** sound (/**k**/ sound) when it's a final consonant.

If you already own *Learning Thai, Your Great Adventure*, then you'll know that not all consonants have a different initial and final [consonant] sound. Some only have one sound. Where this is the case, our picture title only has one word. **One word = one sound**. It couldn't get any easier could it?

This means that if you see this consonant, it **always** makes the same sound irrespective of where it is in a syllable. You'll see the image, you'll remember the title, et voila, you have the consonant sound.

For our next example, we have this consonant: ฯ .

We also have a picture of a kangaroo:

Can you guess the sound this consonant makes?

If we superimpose our consonant shape (ฯ) onto the picture we see that the actual consonant shape conforms to the shape of our **K**angaroo:

There is only one word so this consonant **always** makes the /**k**/ sound, whether it is an initial or a final consonant.

Class of Consonant

The only other thing you have to remember about a consonant is its class. **Every** consonant belongs to one of three classes: High, Middle or Low. How can we remember which consonant is in which class? Again, we have a plan.

If you have *LTYGA* you'll have already seen this.

Every consonant picture will have a background and it will be either red, yellow or green. Each colour corresponds to one of the consonant classes. You may be thinking you'll never be able to remember this. I think you're wrong and don't think you'll ever forget it:

So there you have it:

- **Red** is High Class.
- **Yellow** is Middle Class (I know this is orange but yellow doesn't stand out on a white page; where you see orange, please assume yellow).
- **Green** is Low Class.

Now, with our hero in the first example, we know he's a Middle Class consonant so he'll need a yellow background.

Imagine Galahad Knight in the desert and following what we already know:

1. Initial Consonant sound = /**g**/ (**G**alahad)
2. Final consonant sound = /**k**/ (**K**night.)
3. Consonant class/background: Yellow = Middle Class consonant.

With our antipodean friend, we see him bounding across the Australian outback with the sun setting over a scorching desert.

Here we have:

- **K**angaroo (one word, one sound)
- Red background = High Class consonant.

Great stuff, only 42 more consonants to go.

How to Use This Book

The consonants have been grouped by consonant class to help you learn and remember them. The Middle Class is the smallest group (with 9 conso-nants); then the High Class group (with 11) and then the Low Class (with 24). The consonant groups will be in this order.

I recommend downloading the *Flash Cards* and printing out the Middle Class consonants. You can download the flash cards at:

http://www.learnthaialphabet.com/wp-content/uploads/2012/08/flashcards.pdf

When you have these, cut them along the border lines, put them in one pile (in the order that they're in) and to one side.

Then, go to page 11 and start with the Middle Class consonants. Go through these slowly, one at a time, repeating the picture title (out loud if possible). Do this three or four times then move onto the next picture.

Go through the Middle Class consonants two or three times then put the book to one side. Pick up your flash cards and turn the top one over. Now you see the consonant shape you should be able to recall the picture **and** its name. Repeat the name of it, et voila, you've just recalled the name. Remember the picture background? What colour was it? Now you know its class. Repeat this until you've finished the Middle Class then move onto the High Class and so forth. Once you've been through them all, jumble your flash cards up and practise, practise, practise.

I'm confident that you can learn the consonants in as little as a couple of hours but, as always, it depends on the individual and their learning ability.

I do remember when I started learning Thai that some books (phrase books or otherwise) didn't have the complete list of consonants in the book and that is, to me, just ridiculous. As such, the full list of consonants is in Appendix A at the back of this book.

Before we move onto the alphabet, we'll just have a look at our Learn Thai Alphabet Application.

The Learn Thai Alphabet Application

The Learn Thai Alphabet application is web-based app and works on either the PC or a MAC (plus it works on the iPad 2+). It is based on this book but has interactive quizzes, hints and tips, all the alphabet sounds by native Thai speakers, and much more. If you prefer a more interactive learning experience, then this is for you.

Some sample screens from the app are shown:

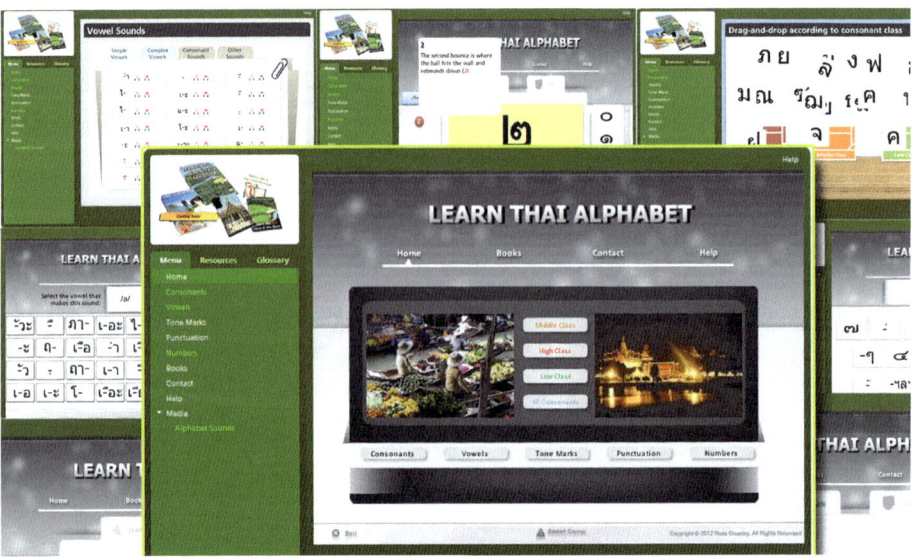

It's available from our website at **www.learnthaialphabet.com**.

Okay, lets learn the alphabet, Middle class consonants first...

Consonant Sounds

Middle Class Consonants

ก Galahad Knight

= **G**alahad **K**night

Here we have **G**alahad **K**night (**/g/** when the consonant is an initial consonant and **/k/** when it is a final consonant) on a yellow background (denoting it's a Middle Class consonant*)*.

จ Jabberwocky Tail

= **J**abberwocky **T**ail

Here we have a **J**abberwocky [with a long] **T**ail: **/j/** as an initial consonant and **/t/** as a final consonant. The yellow background again denotes a Middle Class consonant.

From hereon, we won't refer to '*as an initial or final consonant*' or to the colour of the background and what it denotes in the explanation text. If you need reminding, re-read the introduction.

Dog Treat

  = **D**og **T**reat

A **D**og sitting on the steps, begging for a **T**reat

Dog Treat

  = **D**og **T**reat

Again, the same **D**og begging for another **T**reat

 Damsel Tower

 = **D**amsel **T**ower

A young **D**amsel, alone in a **T**ower

ต Damsel Tower

= **D**amsel **T**ower

The same **D**amsel alone in a [slightly different shaped] **T**ower

บ Bald Patch

= **B**ald **P**atch

A man with a **B**ald **P**atch thinking about going for a paddle

ป – Bottom Pit

= **B**ottom **P**it

A man sitting at the **B**ottom of a **P**it

อ Awful

= **Aw**ful

Staring out of the window at the **Aw**ful weather

High Class Consonants

ข Kangaroo

= **K**angaroo

A **K**angaroo against a red setting sky (**Red** background = **High Class**)

ฃ Karaoke

= **K**araoke

A lady singing **K**araoke down by the marina

ฌ Cat's Tail

= **Ch**at's **T**ail

If you know any French, their word for cat is chat. And with it's long tail we have **Ch**at's **T**ail

ฐ Tassles

= **T**assles

The **T**assles on a Greek Hoplites' helmet

ถ Tails

= **T**ails

A gentleman in **T**ails at the ball

ฬ Profit

 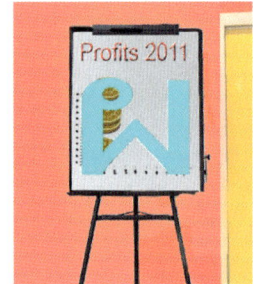

= **P**rofit

The **P**rofit sheet of a business

ฬ Fruit Picking

= **F**ruit **P**icking

Fruit **P**icking berries

ศ Sign Top

= **S**ign **T**op

Follow the **S**ign to the **T**op

ษ Sea Trip

= **S**ea **T**rip

Sea **T**rip

ส Squirrel Tail

= **S**quirrel **T**ail

A **S**quirrel with a long **T**ail eating a nut

ห Humps

= **H**umps

Humps

Low Class Consonants

ค Koala

  = **K**oala

A **K**oala holding onto the branch of a tree (**Green** background = **Low Class**)

ฅ Koala

  = **K**oala

Another **K**oala

ฆ Kite

  = **K**ite

Kite

ง Guarding

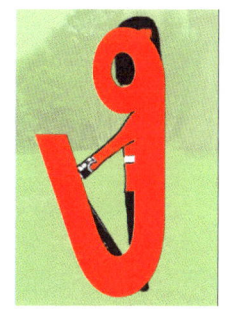

= guardiNG

guardiNG - this consonant makes the **/ng/** sound

ฉ Chef Tasting

= Chef Tasting

Chef **T**asting

ช Sax Twins

= Sax Twins

The **S**axophone **T**wins

ฌ Child Tantrum

 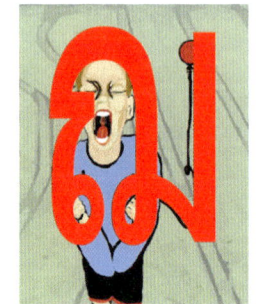

= **Ch**ild **T**antrum

A **Ch**ild having a **T**antrum

ญ You're Nicked

= **Y**ou're **N**icked

"**Y**ou're **N**icked!"

ฏ Tortoise

= **T**ortoise

A cute little **T**ortoise

ฒ Training

= **T**raining

Training

ณ Napoleon

= **N**apoleon

Napoleon

ท Typist

= **T**ypist

Typist

ธ Teabag

= **T**eabag

Teabag

น Navigating

 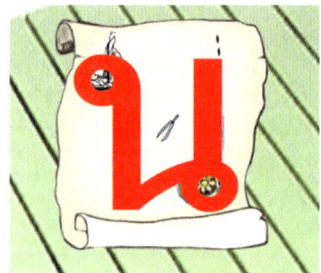

= **N**avigating

[Planning a sailing trip] **N**avigating

พ Praying

= **P**raying

Praying

พ Finished Picking

 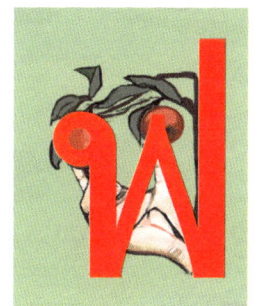

= Finished **P**icking

Back for more berries but I think he's **F**inished **P**icking.

ภ Painting

= Painting

Painting

ม Map

= Map

Two General's planning on a **M**ap

ย Yeti Ice

= **Y**eti **I**ce

A **Y**eti on **I**ce [skates]

ร Rabbit Nibbling

= **R**abbit **N**ibbling

A **R**abbit **Ni**bbling at a small carrot

ล Large Nugget

= **L**arge **N**ugget

"Yeeee, haaaa!" Struck Gold! This prospector has found a **L**arge **N**ugget.

ว Wave over

  = **W**ave **O**ver

"*Where did that come from!*" A large **W**ave **O**ver the bow of the boat.

ฬ Look Nice

  = **L**ook **N**ice

A pretty young lady making herself **L**ook **N**ice

อ Hooray

  = **H**ooray

I think he's just won? "**H**ooray!"

Vowel Sounds

Simple Vowels

Well done for working your way through the consonant sounds, now we'll look at the vowels.

Unlike consonant sounds, vowels don't belong to any class so you only have to remember the sounds they make.

Please bear in mind that the sounds these vowels make (from the pictures) are as close as the English language allows us to get to the actual Thai sound. We have checked and verified all these using the Cambridge phonetic system.

Thai uses two types of vowel: short vowels and long vowels. With the transliteration system that we use in the book *Learning Thai, Your Great Adventure* we differentiate between short and long vowels by doubling up on the vowel when it is long. For example, when you see the drawing *bed*, even though the sound is the /e/ part of *bed*, the actual Thai sound we are trying to produce/replicate is a long vowel and, as it's a long vowel, we double-up when we write it: /ee/. Please note though, it is still pronounced /e/ it's just a longer, drawn-out sound. I hope that hasn't confused you too much. So, without further ado:

- ำ = This vowel makes the /**am**/ sound as in **um**brella

ไ - = This vowel makes the /**ai**/ sound as in kn**i**ght.

ໄ - = /**ai**/ as in fl**y**.

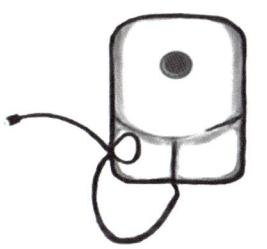 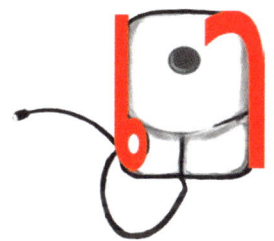

ໄ - ໆ = /**ou**/ as in m**ou**se

- ໃ = /**a**/ as in p**u**ffin

- ꓨ = /**aa**/ as in p**a**lm

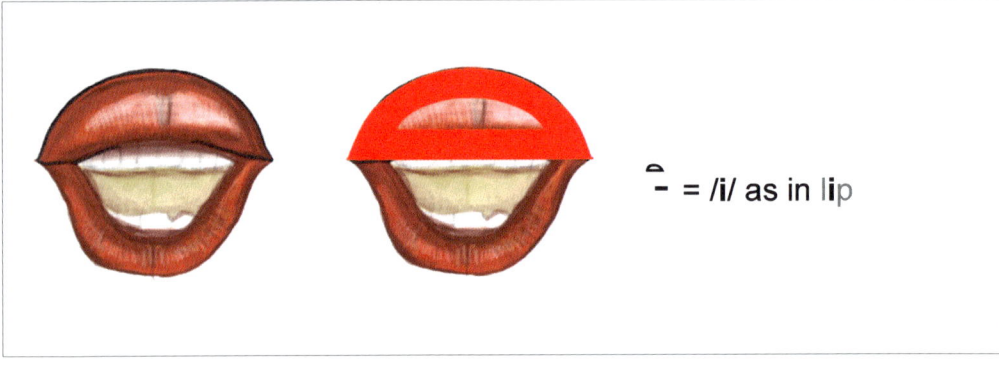

꙼ = /**i**/ as in l**i**p

꙼ = /**ii**/ as in st**ee**ple

ُ = /u̇/ as in p**u**sh-up

ُ = /ʉʉ/ as in bl**oo**m

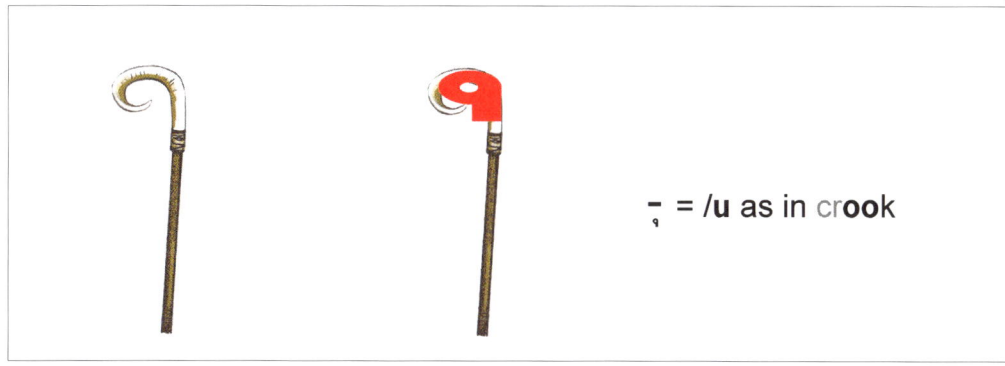

ٜ = /u as in cr**oo**k

ʊ = /uu/ as in b**oo**t

 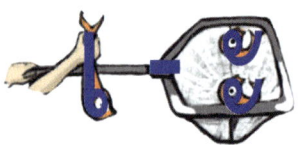

ɭ - ʊ = /e/ as in n**e**t

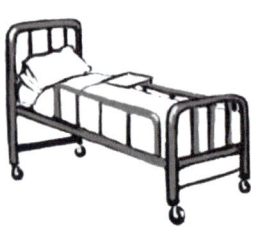 

ɭ - = /ee/ as in b**e**d

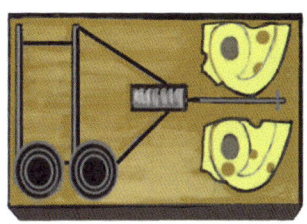 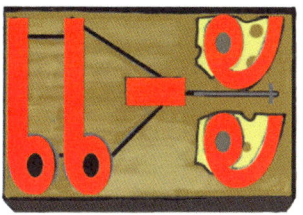 ᒪᒪ – ᴗ = /ɛ/ as in trap

  ᒪᒪ – = /ɛɛ/ as in mare

  ᒋ – ᴗ = /o/ as in cot

โ - = /oo/ as in gh**o**st

เ - าะ = /ɔ/ as in sl**o**t

- อ = /ɔɔ/ as in **aw**ful

You may have noticed that this vowel (อ) is also a consonant, it is. Whichever function or role it is providing, it still makes the same sound. For further explanation you'll need *Learning Thai, Your Great Adventure.*

That concludes the simple vowels, now we'll have a look at the complex vowels.

Complex Vowels

When we refer to complex vowels we mean vowels which are composed of more than one sound, i.e. dipthongs or tripthongs (two or three sounds respectively). We have quite a few dipthongs in the English language but not too many tripthongs, Thai has a few more. Thank you in advance for bearing with my diagrams and descriptions below, it took me quite a while to come up with the right pictures that would accurately represent the sounds and the vowel shapes; I hope they help you

เ - อ = /əə/ as in **ear**ly

เ◌ีย = /iiə/ as in rein**deer**

เ◌ือ = /ɯɯə/ as in sk**ua**

◌ัว = /ua/ as in p**ur**e

ฤ - = /rɨ/ as in **roo**k

ฤๅ - = /rɨɨ/ as in **roo**t

ฦ - = /lɨ/ as in **loo**kout

ฦๅ - = /lɨɨ/ as in **loo**ney

Where to Write Vowels

As you probably know, and are perhaps confused by, Thai vowels are written before, above, after and below consonants. Shock, gasp, horror, scared? Don't be, it's very straightforward.

With few exceptions (four to be precise: ไ -, ◌ ̃, ฦ -, ฦๅ -), when a vowel contains a loop, it <u>always</u> points in the direction of where the consonant is written. So, when you see เ it points to the right. This means the consonant is written to the right of it (the vowel): เ -.

Vowels Before

These vowels all have loops that point **at** the consonant; therefore, these are written to the left (in front) of the consonant they 'belong' to:

เ -, แ -, ไ -, โ -, ฤ -, ฤๅ -

Vowels Below

These two vowels have loops that point up, so they are written underneath the consonant they 'belong to':

◌̣ , ◌̤ (I've drawn these much larger than those shown previously you can see them clearly).

Vowels Above

Vowels that are written above the consonants need to have a base, and preferably a flat base; four out of the five do. I like to think that the fifth one 'is getting there: one day it will be flat, but it isn't hasn't made it just yet:

◌̄ , ◌̄, ◌̄, ◌̄ ◌̆   This last vowel (◌̆) is not shown in this book as it's the same as this vowel, - ะ , just written in a different position. We don't cover it here but it's explained in *Learning Thai, Your Great Adventure* (section 7.3).

Vowels After

Those vowels that come after the consonant always point (with the curved bit) at the consonant. Remember that the loops point 'at' the consonant:

-ำ ,- า , - ะ

Note, where a consonant is used as part of a complex vowel, it is always written after the consonant the vowel belongs to.

That's it, that's all the vowels. Remember, the individual vowel components are **always** written in the same place.

Also remember, that you can download all the flash cards at:

http://www.learnthaialphabet.com/wp-content/uploads/2012/08/flashcards.pdf

Tone

Thai is a tonal language and every syllable will have one of five tones: high, low, middle, falling or rising.

Because the Thai language is tonal, changing the tone of a syllable or a word changes it's meaning. You now know that more than one consonant makes the /**ch**/ sound, the /**s**/ sound, the /**p**/ sound, etc. So how do we actually know which consonant to use?

Well this is one of the difficulties with learning Thai, especially learning to write Thai. The vowels are fairly straightforward but the fact that within a consonant **class** there are sometimes more than one consonant making a particular sound, this can prove difficult. Ultimately, you have to learn each individual word. It is a laborious process but not insurmountable by any means. Children do it, why can't we?

Before we look into this, we need to know that there are four factors that affect syllable tone, these are:

1. Does the syllable have a tone mark above the initial consonant?
2. What is the class of the consonant (remember, each consonant must belong to either High, Middle or Low class)?
3. Is the vowel length long or short?
4. Does the end [consonant] sound make this a *live syllable* or a *dead syllable* (refer to *Learning Thai, Your Great Adventure*, section 5.3)?

Point number 1, is the overriding factor here. If the syllable has a tone mark, forget about the other rules.

Tone Marks

There are four tone marks in Thai script and these marks in conjunction with the consonant class help determine what the syllable tone is. This is as follows:

Tone Mark	When written above the consonant class (shown below), that syllable will produce the tone shown:		
	Low Class	Middle Class	High Class
่	Falling Tone (^)	Low (\\)	Low (\\)
้	High Tone (/)	Falling (^)	Falling (^)
๊	High (/)		
๋	Rising Tone (v)		

How To Use the Table

If your syllable has one of the above tone marks above the initial consonant, you then need to identify the consonant class of the initial consonant (High, Middle or Low class). Once you have done this, you cross reference it in the table to get the syllable tone.

Some of you may think that this is difficult to remember (for me it was) so I came up with the following pictures and text to help me.

Remembering Tone Mark Rules

Mái èek (⁻)

This looks like a bomb dropped from a warplane.

- When the plane flies on **high** or **middle** altitude bombing missions (*high* or *middle* class consonants) the bomb explodes at **low level** (read *low tone*).

- When the plane is on a **low** altitude bombing mission (read *low* class consonant) it uses pinpoint accuracy and can drop the bomb into holes and the bomb **falls** deeper into the ground (read *falling* tone).

Therefore:

Middle & **High** [class consonants] = **Low** [tone]; **Low** [class consonant] = **Fall**ing [tone].

Mái too (˘)

Imagine this as the head of a sickle (or a scythe) used in a peasant rebellion.

The **low class** peasants revolt and cut the heads off of the **middle** and **high** classes who all **fall** from grace and the **low** classes now elevate themselves to the new, vacant **high** class.

Therefore: **Middle** & **High** = **Fall**ing, **Low** = [the new] **High.**

Picture in your mind the shape of a sickle used in the 1917 Russian Revolution.

Mái dtrii (◌̋)

Imagine this shape as a crown on the head of royalty - the *high*est level (**high** tone with all consonant classes).

Mái jàt-dtà-waa (◌̌)

This is like a *rising* star, twinkling in the night sky (**rise** [ing] tone with all consonant classes).

That's much easier to remember! But, how do we determine tone if there isn't a tone mark?

Determining Tone

If the syllable doesn't have a tone mark then you have to calculate the syllable tone. This is one of the things that puts people off learning the language as it can be very difficult (and slow) to work out the tone of each syllable: it doesn't have to be though; but, before we show you the easy way, we'll go through the standard method. First of all, we'll reiterate on what information we need.

Here are the factors that you need to know to calculate a syllable tone:

1. The class of the consonant

2. Whether the vowel is short or long, and

3. Whether the final consonant is a *sonorant* or *stop* final (refer to Appendix C).

Syllable Type	Consonant Class		
	High Class	**Middle Class**	**Low Class**
Dead Syllables	Low Tone (\\)	Low Tone (\\)	Short Vowel: High Tone (/)
			Long Vowel: Falling Tone (^)
Live Syllables	Rising Tone (v)	Middle Tone	Middle Tone

As you can see from the table above, *for Low Class consonants only*, if the syllable is dead, the tone will depend on whether the vowel is short or long.

Complicated? Of course it is. It's also very difficult to work out - this way. But, as always, I have a much easier method to help you and that is by remembering a few simple acronyms.

Remembering How to Calculate Tone

Here are the ones that I use to remember the tone rules:

*   **H**arry **D**rinks **L**ager (**H**igh [class consonant] + **D**ead [syllable] = **L**ow [tone]) **HDL**
*   **H**arry **L**ikes **R**ed Stripe (**H**igh + **L**ive = **R**ising) **HLR**
*   **M**ike **D**rinks **L**ager (**M**iddle + **D**ead = **L**ow) **MDL**
*   **M**ike **L**ikes **M**iller (**M**iddle + **L**ive = **M**iddle) **MLM**
*   **L**esley **D**rinks **SH**andy (**L**ow + **D**ead + **S**hort [vowel] = **H**igh) **LDSH**
*   **L**esley **D**rinks **L**ager **F**ast (**L**ow + **D**ead + **L**ong [vowel] = **F**alling) **LDLF**
*   **L**esley **L**ikes **M**iller (**L**ow + **L**ive = **M**iddle) **LLM**

Remember these and you'll never have to refer to the table again.[1]

---

[1] Now you've probably noticed that these acronyms have a slight alcoholic slant towards them. The reason for this is it helps me remember them (the acronyms, not the alcohol). It is actually a proven fact that the more raunchy or saucier the link is between the item you are trying to remember and the story, picture or aid you use to actually remember it is, the easier it is to recall.

Appendices

Appendix A. Consonant List

I've included the list of consonants that you've gone through here so that you can see the order they're actually in and the sounds they make. You can use this as a quick reference table. Refer to Appendix H for the actual table with Thai names, what the actual name means, etc.

No.	Thai Character	Picture Name	Initial Consonant Sound	Final Consonant Sound
1	ก	Galahad Knight	/g/	/k/
2	ข	Kangaroo	/k/	
3	ฃ	Karaoke	/k/	
4	ค	Koala	/k/	
5	ฅ	Koala	/k/	
6	ฆ	Kite	/k/	
7	ง	guardiNG	/ng/	
8	จ	Jabberwocky Tail	/j/	/t/
9	ฉ	Chat Tail	/ch/	/t/
10	ช	Chef Tasting	/ch/	/t/
11	ซ	Saxophone Twins	/s/	/t/
12	ฌ	Child Tantrum	/ch/	/t/
13	ญ	You're Nicked	/y/	/n/
14	ฎ	Dog Treat	/d/	/t/
15	ฏ	Dog Treat	/dt/	/t/
16	ฐ	Tassles	/t/	
17	ฑ	Tortoise	/t/	
18	ฒ	Training	/t/	
19	ณ	Napoleon	/n/	

20	ด	Damsel Tower	/d/	/t/
21	ต	Damsel Tower	/dt/	/t/
22	ถ	Tails	/t/	
23	ท	Typist	/t/	
24	ธ	Teabag	/t/	
25	น	Navigating	/n/	
26	บ	Bald Patch	/b/	/p/
27	ป	Bottom Pit	/bp/	/p/
28	ผ	Profits	/p/	
29	ฝ	Fruit Picking	/f/	/p/
30	พ	Praying	/p/	
31	ฟ	Finished Picking	/f/	/p/
32	ภ	Painting	/p/	
33	ม	Map	/m/	
34	ย	Yeti Ice	/y/	/i/
35	ร	Rabbit Nibbling	/r/	/n/
36	ล	Large Nugget	/l/	/n/
37	ว	Wave Over	/w/	/o/
38	ศ	Sign Top	/s/	/t/
39	ษ	Sea Trip	/s/	/t/
40	ส	Squirrel Tail	/s/	/t/
41	ห	Humps	/h/	
42	ฬ	Look Nice	/l/	/n/
43	อ	Awful	/ɔɔ/	
44	ฮ	Hooray	/h/	

Appendix A.1 Patterns

You will be able to see some patterns in the initial and final consonant sounds in the above table:

* If the initial consonant sound is /ch/, /d/ or /s/ the final consonant sound is /t/
* If the initial consonant sound is /b/ or /f/, the final consonant sound is /p/
* If the initial consonant sound is /l/ or /r/, the final consonant sound is /n/.

Appendix B. Different Consonant Sounds

There are three consonants which, when they are in the *initial consonant* position, have no direct English equivalent, these are (in the drawings): ฎ (Dog Treat), ต (Damsel Tower) and ป (Bottom Pit).

The sounds are very similar to ฎ (Dog Treat), ด (Damsel Tower) and ป (Bald Patch) but are formed by two consonants pronounced together:

* ฎ (Dog Treat) = /dt/ (as in stop)
* ต (Damsel Tower) = /dt/ (as in stop)
* ป (Bottom Pit) = /bp/ (as in spot)

as opposed to:

* ฎ (Dog Treat) = /d/ (as in dog)
* ด (Damsel Tower) = /d/ (as in dog)
* บ (Bald Patch) = /b/ (as in ball)

At this stage, just recognising the consonants and associating the /d/ or /b/ sound is where you want to be; once you've got that, then work on the finer points above.

Appendix C. Stop or Sonorant Final Sounds

There are 8 final consonant sounds. Five of these are sonorant and three are stop final sounds. If you remember the stop final sounds, the remainder are all sonorant finals. The stop final consonant sounds are /k/, /p/ and /t/.

I know you can say the sound and work out if your larynx vibrates but I use the following phrase to help me:

Stop eating KP nuts as they stick in your Teeth.

Appendix D. Missing Vowels

For the purists among you, you will notice that we've only included 28 drawings for the vowels yet there are 32 vowels in the Thai language.

The main reason for this is that the excluded vowels are <u>very uncommon</u>; the secondary reason is I couldn't come up with an appropriate image for them. The remaining four are:

เ - อะ - this produces the /ə/ sound as in **a**bove

เ - ยะ - this vowel makes the /ia/ sound as in r**ia**

เ - อะ - this one makes the /ʉa/ sound, as is the word n**ew**er

- วะ - the last vowel makes the /ua/ sound as in b**ua**t.

Appendix E. Numbers

Unless you go off the beaten track in Thailand, you are likely to see familiar Arabic numerals (0 - 9). If you're in an area where English is not particularly common then it will help you to know what the Thai numerals actually are. Some places have a dual pricing structure where tourists pay more than Thai's, that's just the way it is; if this bothers you then you have the choice of voting with your feet. It used to bother me at first until, on one trip, I saw an American guy who produced his Thai work permit when told what the entry fee was; subsequently, he was charged the Thai price.

Here are the Thai numerals 0 - 9. Learn them for what it's worth but I don't have any pictures or diagrams for these

๐	0	๕	5
๑	1	๖	6
๒	2	๗	7
๓	3	๘	8
๔	4	๙	9

Appendix F. Special Signs & Features

The Thai language has few punctuation marks or other 'signs'. The ones that you will see are shown below:

ๆ	When you see this, it means the previous word needs to be repeated.
ฯ	This sign means that the preceding word is an abbreviation.
◌์	This sign makes the letter it is above silent.
ฯลฯ	This sign has the same effect as 'etc' does in the English language.

Appendix G. Flash Cards

I haven't enclosed the flash cards at the back of this book as I really don't like damaging books. I have posted them to the following location where you can download as many times as you wish:

http://www.learnthaialphabet.com/wp-content/uploads/2012/08/flashcards.pdf

Appendix H. Full List of Consonants and Their Meaning

Once you've progressed past the consonant sounds, classes, vowel sounds, tone marks, etc., you're probably going to want to learn the actual consonant names. I wouldn't do this until you're sure you're ready: the sounds are far more important at the early stage but it's handy to know the consonant names as you progress.

First, if you ask or someone asks you how to spell a word; and, secondly, if you want to use a Thai dictionary. One thing which very few books will help you with is the consonant order. With the English alphabet we consider it simple, "*A, B, C, D, E, F...*" and so forth, with the Thai alphabet this is not so: consonants and vowels are not mixed.

This is what gave me the idea for *Learning Thai, Your Great Adventure* (and that book gave me the idea for this book). I simply couldn't remember the consonant order. There were no books that address this, mine does. If you really want to learn to speak, read and write Thai, then I would, of course, thoroughly recommend that book to you.

We are also gradually getting more and more videos onto the website to help you with sounds, pronunciation, etc. We will add to these in due course.

No.	Thai Consonant	Transliterated Thai Name	Meaning	Initial Consonant Sound	Final Consonant Sound
1	ก ไก่	Gɔɔ Gài	Chicken	/g/	/k/
2	ข ไข่	Ǩɔɔ Kài	Egg	/k/	
3	ฃ ขวด	Ǩɔɔ Kùat	Bottle	/k/	
4	ค ควาย	Kɔɔ Kwaai	Buffalo	/k/	
5	ฅ คน	Kɔɔ Kon	Person	/k/	
6	ฆ ระฆัง	Kɔɔ Rá-kang	Bell	/k/	
7	ง งู	Ngɔɔ Nguu	Snake	/ng/	
8	จ จาน	Jɔɔ Jaan	Plate	/j/	/t/
9	ฉ ฉิ่ง	Cȟɔɔ Chìng	Cymbals	/ch/	/t/
10	ช ช้าง	Chɔɔ Cháang	Elephant	/ch/	/t/
11	ซ โซ่	Sɔɔ Sôo	Chain	/s/	/t/
12	ฌ เฌอ	Chɔɔ Chəə	Tree	/ch/	/t/
13	ญ หญิง	Yɔɔ Yǐng	Woman	/y/	/n/
14	ฎ ชฎา	Dɔɔ Chá-daa	Head-dress	/d/	/t/
15	ฏ ปฏัก	Dtɔɔ Bpà-dtàk	Spear	/dt/	/t/
16	ฐ ฐาน	Ťɔɔ Tǎan	Pedestal	/t/	
17	ฑ มณโฑ	Tɔɔ Montoo	Giant's Wife	/t/	
18	ฒ ผู้เฒ่า	Tɔɔ Pûu-tâo	Old Man	/t/	
19	ณ เณร	Nɔɔ Neen	Monk	/n/	
20	ด เด็ก	Dɔɔ Dèk	Child	/d/	/t/
21	ต เต่า	Dtɔɔ Dtào	Turtle	/dt/	/t/
22	ถ ถุง	Ťɔɔ Tǔng	Bag	/t/	

23	ท ทหาร	Tɔɔ Tá-hǎan	Soldier	/t/	
24	ธ ธง	Tɔɔ Tong	Flag	/t/	
25	น หนู	Nɔɔ Nǔu	Mouse	/n/	
26	บ ใบไม้	Bɔɔ Bai-mái	Leaf	/b/	/p/
27	ป ปลา	Bpɔɔ Bplaa	Fish	/bp/	/p/
28	ผ ผึ้ง	Pɔɔ Pɯng	Bee	/p/	
29	ฝ ฝา	Fɔɔ Fǎa	Lid	/f/	/p/
30	พ พาน	Pɔɔ Paan	Tray	/p/	
31	ฟ ฟัน	Fɔɔ Fan	Tooth	/f/	/p/
32	ภ สำเภา	Pɔɔ Sǎmpao	Junk	/p/	
33	ม ม้า	Mɔɔ Máa	Horse	/m/	
34	ย ยักษ์	Yɔɔ Yák	Giant	/y/	/i/
35	ร เรือ	Rɔɔ Rɯɯa	Boat	/r/	/n/
36	ล ลิง	Lɔɔ Ling	Monkey	/l/	/n/
37	ว แหวน	Wɔɔ Wɛ̌ɛn	Ring	/w/	/o/
38	ศ ศาลา	Sɔ̌ɔ Sǎa-laa	Tent	/s/	/t/
39	ษ ฤาษี	Sɔ̌ɔ Rɯɯ-sǐi	Hermit	/s/	/t/
40	ส เสือ	Sɔ̌ɔ Sɯ̌ɯa	Tiger	/s/	/t/
41	ห หีบ	Hɔ̌ɔ Hìip	Chest	/h/	
42	ฬ จุฬา	Lɔɔ Jù-laa	Star-shaped Kite	/l/	/n/
43	อ อ่าง	ɔɔ Àang	Bowl	/ɔɔ/	
44	ฮ นกฮูก	Hɔɔ Nók-hûuk	Owl	/h/	

Appendix I. Full List of Vowels

The following tables show the full list of vowels:

Appendix I.1 Simple Vowels

Short Vowel			Long Vowel		
Vowel	**Sound**	**Sounds Like**	**Vowel**	**Sound**	**Sounds Like**
The 4 vowels to the right can be short or long but are considered long for tone purposes.			-ํา	/am/	umbrella
			ใ -	/ai/	knight
			ไ -	/ai/	fly
			เ - า	/ao/	mouse
- ะ	/a/	puffin	- า	/aa/	palm
◌ิ	/i/	lip	◌ี	/ii/	steeple
◌ึ	/ʉ/	push-up	◌ื	/ʉʉ/	bloom
◌ุ	/u/	crook	◌ู	/uu/	boot
เ - ะ	/e/	net	เ -	/ee/	bed
แ - ะ	/ɛ/	trap	แ -	/ɛɛ/	mare
โ - ะ	/o/	cot	โ -	/oo/	ghost
เ - าะ	/ɔ/	slot	- อ	/ɔɔ/	awful

Appendix I.2 Complex Vowels

Short Vowel			Long Vowel		
Vowel	**Sound**	**Sounds Like**	**Vowel**	**Sound**	**Sounds Like**
เ - อะ	/ə/	above	เ - อ	/əə/	early
เ◌ียะ	/ia/	ria	เ◌ีย	/iia/	reindeer
เ◌ือะ	/ʉa/	newer	เ◌ือ	/ʉʉa/	Skua
◌ัวะ	/ua/	buat	◌ัว	/uua/	pure
ฤ	/rʉ/	rook	ฤา	/rʉʉ/	root
ฦ	/lʉ/	lookout	ฦา	/lʉʉ/	looney

Printed in Great Britain
by Amazon.co.uk, Ltd.,
Marston Gate.